PLEASE BE PATIENT WITH ME
AND MY ADHD

My name is David and I have ADHD. That stands for Attention-Deficit Hyperactivity Disorder. I face challenges daily and things can become very overwhelming for me.

It is hard for me to complete simple tasks. When I have multiple things to do, sometimes I don't know where to begin.

Cleaning my room can take forever! When I see so many things on the floor my brain goes into overload. Then I start to panic!

When I am at school sometimes my teacher gets upset with me because I squirm and move around in my seat. I don't do it on purpose, but it is so hard to focus and keep still when I am thinking about so many things!

classroom

When I am at home my mom and dad do their best to help me stay on task. It is most helpful when they create a to do list and hang it up for me to see.

Even when I am on task, I still face challenges. Sometimes I am so into what I am doing I lose track of time!

I can't believe I missed the school bus

I feel like I live in a world of my own because sometimes others don't understand why I am different.

Then I realize that ADHD is a part of me,
and it is nothing to be ashamed of.

I have a family that loves me so much!
They are always there to support me
no matter what.

Facing challenges and overcoming obstacles makes me feel like a superhero. I really love being me! So please, be patient with my ADHD.